Famous Finds

Written by Mary-Anne Creasy

Flying Start
to Literacy®

Contents

Introduction   4

Chapter 1 Mary Anning, fossil hunter   6

Who was Mary Anning?   10

Chapter 2 Tutankhamen's Tomb   16

Searching for Tutankhamen   18

One last dig   20

Inside the tomb   22

The biggest treasure trove ever   24

Conclusion   26

Glossary   27

Index   28

Introduction

Imagine finding a dinosaur **fossil** or hidden treasure. What would you do?

Many people are fascinated by the idea of discovery. They dream of discovering a new species of animal, or ancient fossils or buried treasure.

And many people have made some amazing and important discoveries. For some people, their discoveries made them both rich and famous. But others were not recognised until after they had died.

The stories about how these people made their discoveries are just as fascinating as the discoveries themselves.

Chapter 1

Mary Anning, fossil hunter

South coast of England, about 200 years ago

Mary Anning walked carefully along the beach close to the cliffs. She was with her brother, Joseph. There had been a storm the previous day and rain and wind had loosened the rocks and soil on the cliffs. They knew there was the danger of a **landslide**.

Mary kept her eyes focused on the ground, looking for **fossils**. Suddenly she heard a rumble and looked up. Rocks and soil were falling down the cliff face.

"Mary, quick!" said Joseph.

He grabbed his sister's hand. Together they ran towards the sea where they were safe, away from the tumbling rocks.

They watched as the cliffs crumbled and rocks bounced onto the beach.

Mary Anning and her brother searched for fossils near the cliffs along the coast in the south of England.

After the landslide, Mary and Joseph walked back to the cliffs.

As they got closer, Joseph could see something, a smooth rock sticking out of the cliff face. They quickly opened their bags and grabbed their tools. Joseph scraped away at the flaky stone and soil, while Mary tapped around the rock.

She was slow and careful. In her mind, she heard her father's voice:

"Take your time, Mary, these rocks have been here for a long time and they aren't going anywhere."

Drawing of the ichthyosaurus skeleton

Over many hours, 12-year-old Mary and her 15-year-old brother uncovered the skull of a strange beast. They didn't know what it was, but they thought it was a crocodile.

A few months later, in the same area, Mary discovered a huge skeleton. It belonged to the skull they had found. It was identified as the skeleton of a dinosaur.

Mary's discovery marked the beginning of her remarkable life as a fossil hunter.

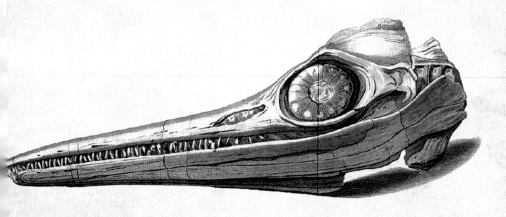

Skull of the ichthyosaurus found by Joseph and Mary Anning.

Who was Mary Anning?

Mary Anning was born in 1799. Mary was one of nine children, but only she and Joseph lived past childhood.

Mary and Joseph's father was a furniture maker, but his real passion was searching for fossils in the cliffs along the coast. He sold the fossils he found to tourists and collectors to make extra money for his family.

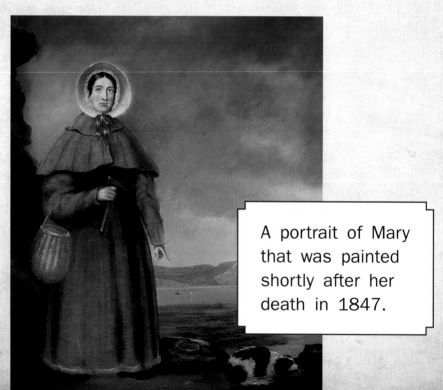

A portrait of Mary that was painted shortly after her death in 1847.

This beach is close to where Mary and her family lived.
It is famous for its fossils.

When they were young, Mary and Joseph often joined their father as he searched for fossils on the beach near their home. He taught them how to find and identify fossils.

Soon, they were finding their own fossils.

11

When Mary was ten years old, her father died. Not only did the family have no money, but Mr Anning had left an enormous **debt**. The family sometimes had to rely on other people to give them food and shelter.

As soon as Joseph was old enough, he began to learn a **trade** to help earn money for the family. Mary continued to hunt fossils on her own and she found many dinosaur skeletons.

Like most girls at that time, Mary did not go to school. But she had always been curious and loved learning. Mary taught herself to read and write, and she also learnt maths and some science. And she could draw.

She wrote about the fossils that she found on the beach and drew accurate pictures of her discoveries.

Opposite page: Mary kept a journal in which she wrote about and drew the fossils she found.

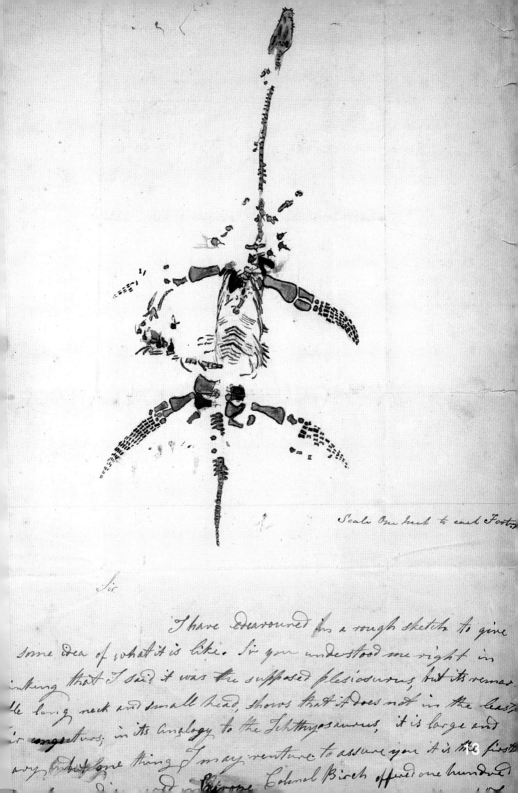

Scale One Inch to each Foot

Sir

I have endeavoured by a rough sketch to give some idea of what it is like. Sir you understood me right in thinking that I said it was the supposed plesiosaurus, but its remarkable long neck and small head, shows that it does not in the least its congestios, in its analogy to the Ichthyosaurus, it is large and very but one thing I may venture to assure you it is the first Colonel Birch offered one hundred

13

Mary went on to find so many amazing fossils that her discoveries became well known in the science world. Because of her knowledge and experience, collectors and scientists from around the world came to her for advice. Mary often helped them find fossils.

Most scientists at that time were wealthy men, and they formed clubs to discuss new discoveries. But these clubs were only for men.

Ammonite fossils were some of the many different types of fossils that Mary found and sold.

Visitors to the Natural History Museum
in London can see the fossils Mary found.

Although Mary had discovered many dinosaur
skeletons, she was never invited to join a club,
give a talk or even attend a meeting. The
scientists often wrote about Mary's discoveries
without even mentioning her name.

When Mary died in 1847, she had begun
to receive some recognition as a valuable
contributor to scientific knowledge. Today,
she is remembered as one of the greatest
fossil hunters ever.

Chapter 2

Tutankhamen's Tomb

Valley of the Kings, Egypt, 1922

Howard Carter drilled a hole into the dusty stone wall. He was both nervous and excited, and his hands trembled as he drilled.

Finally, the hole was large enough. He held up a candle and looked through the hole. At first, he couldn't see anything – the space was too dark.

Valley of the Kings, Egypt

Howard Carter and his assistant find the door to Tutankhamen's **Tomb**, Egypt, 1922.

But then his eyes adjusted to the darkness of the chamber and he couldn't believe what he saw – the chamber was filled with dazzling objects. Above him, someone called out impatiently:

"Well, what can you see? Anything?"

Carter nodded. "Yes," he stammered, "wonderful things!"

It was 1922, and Howard Carter had just discovered Tutankhamen's Tomb and all its treasures.

17

Searching for Tutankhamen

Howard Carter was an **archaeologist** and had been on many digs in Egypt. Archaeologists had heard that there was a **burial chamber** of a boy king in the famous Valley of the Kings, but no one had ever found it. The boy king was Tutankhamen.

A wealthy man named Lord Carnarvon was certain that if anyone could find Tutankhamen's Tomb, it was Howard Carter. So he paid Carter and his team to dig in the Valley of the Kings.

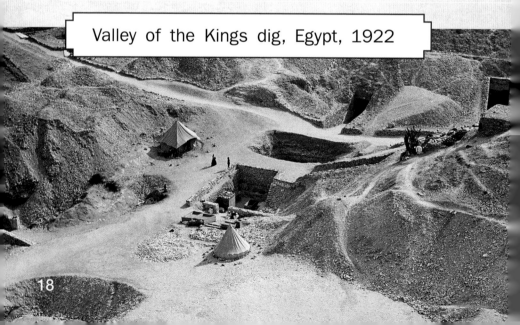

Valley of the Kings dig, Egypt, 1922

Lord Carnarvon

Lord Carnarvon (left) was interested in finding treasures in Egypt, but he did not have the skills of an archaeologist. In 1907, he met Howard Carter (right) in Egypt, and the pair worked together for 17 years. During this time, they found many ancient Egyptian **artifacts**.

At the time, it was common for wealthy people to pay archaeologists to find treasure for them.

But Carter had been digging for six years, without any success. He had discovered three tombs, but they were all empty. The wealthy lord was becoming impatient. He wrote to Carter to say that he was running out of money. He could no longer pay Carter to keep searching.

One last dig

But Carter was convinced that he and his team could find Tutankhamen's burial chamber. He wanted one last chance and was given permission for another dig.

Carter and his team decided to search under some ancient huts. As they were clearing out rubble from around the area, one of Carter's workers stumbled over a large stone. They dug around it and found some steps that went under the huts.

The entrance to the tomb discovered by Carter

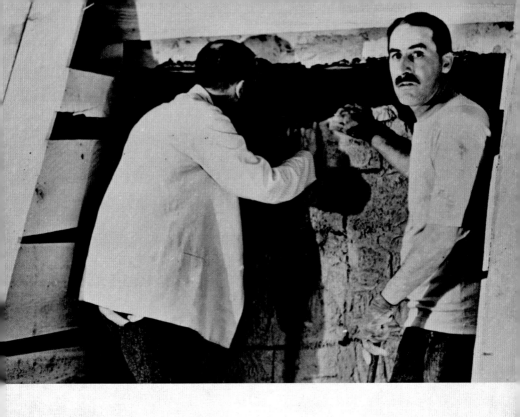

Carter went down the steps, only to discover a
a sealed stone door. He knew Lord Carnarvon
wanted to be there when they opened the door,
so he sent news of their discovery to England.
Then he ordered the stairway to be filled back
in to hide it, so no one else could find it.

It took Lord Carnarvon more than two weeks
to travel from England to Egypt. Finally, he
arrived, and Carter drilled through the stone door.

Inside the tomb

On the day that Howard Carter and Lord Carnarvon finally got inside the chamber, they could see it was filled with gold objects that glinted in the candlelight.

They had discovered the greatest ancient Egyptian treasure ever known.

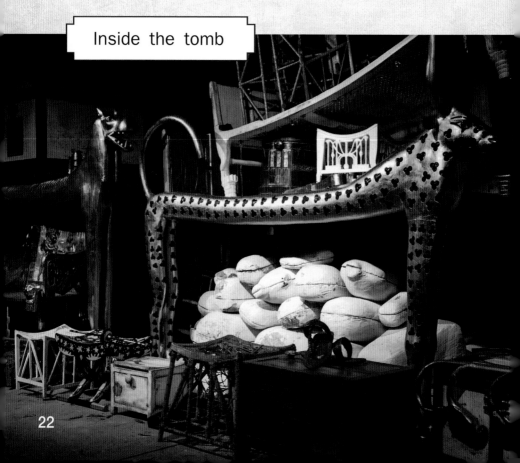

Inside the tomb

Inside Tutankhamen's Tomb

Statues

Chariots

Jewellery

Sarcophagus

Gold throne

The biggest treasure trove ever

It took eight years to list and remove all the objects in the tomb and transport them to Cairo. In all, there were more than 5,000 artifacts. Never before or since has there been such a significant find from any other ancient human civilisation.

Removing treasure from the tomb

Le Petit Journal
illustré

Dans la poussière des Tombeaux
En Egypte, dans la Vallée des Rois, un archéologue anglais découvre une nouvelle sépulture. C'est dans un état de conservation parfaite et remplie encore des objets précieux qu'on y avait déposés, la tombe du pharaon Tut-anh-Amen, endormi depuis trois mille cinq cents ans.

The front page of a French newspaper shows the tomb's discovery.

The discovery of Tutankhamen's Tomb captured the world's imagination – swiftly turning into "Tut-mania." Howard Carter and everyone involved in the find became famous.

Today, we are still fascinated by **ancient Egypt** and Tutankhamen's treasure, and the hunt is still on for more tombs and treasures of the **pharaohs**.

Conclusion

It's easy to see why people become obsessed with searching for hidden treasure – the reward for the effort can be huge.

So, if you have a passion for finding something, and you have the time and determination, you too might make a famous find!

Glossary

ancient Egypt Egypt in the time before 30 BCE

archaeologist a person who studies history by excavating sites and studying artifacts

artifacts objects made by a person

burial chamber a room, usually underground, used for the burial of a human body

debt an amount of money that is owed

fossils the buried remains of a prehistoric animal or plant that have become like rock

landslide a mass of rock or earth sliding down a mountain or cliff

pharaohs rulers in ancient Egypt

tomb an underground place where dead people are buried

trade a job that requires training and manual skills

Index

Anning, Joseph   6–12

Anning, Mary   6–15

archaeologist   18, 19, 27

artifacts   19, 24, 27

burial chamber   18, 20, 27

Carnarvon, Lord   18, 19, 21, 22

Carter, Howard   16–25

dinosaur   4, 9, 12, 15

Egypt   16, 17, 18, 19, 21

fossil   4, 6, 7, 9, 10, 11, 12, 14, 15, 27

scientists   14, 15

skeleton   8, 9, 12, 15

treasure   4, 17, 19, 22, 24, 25, 26

Tutankhamen   18

Tutankhamen's Tomb   16–25

Valley of the Kings   16, 18